BROWN V. BOARD OF EDUCATION

The Case for Integration

by Judith Conaway

BROWN V. BOARD OF EDUCATION

The Case for Integration

by Judith Conaway

Content Adviser: Derek Shouba, History Professor
and Assistant Provost, Roosevelt University

Reading Adviser: Katie Van Sluys, Ph.D.,
School of Education, DePaul University

Compass Point Books ✦ Minneapolis, Minnesota

✦ COMPASS POINT BOOKS

3109 West 50th Street, #115
Minneapolis, MN 55410

Visit Compass Point Books on the Internet at
www.compasspointbooks.com
or e-mail your request to
custserv@compasspointbooks.com

For Compass Point Books
Jennifer VanVoorst, Jaime Martens, XNR Productions, Inc.,
Catherine Neitge, Keith Griffin, and Carol Jones

Produced by White-Thomson Publishing Ltd.

For White-Thomson Publishing
Stephen White-Thomson, Susan Crean, Amy Sparks,
Tinstar Design Ltd., Derek Shouba, Peggy Bresnick Kendler,
Will Hare, and Timothy Griffin

Library of Congress Cataloging-in-Publication Data
Conaway, Judith, 1948–
  Brown v. Board of Education : the case for integration / By Judith
Conaway.
      p. cm. — (Snapshots in history)
  Includes bibliographical references and index.
  ISBN-13: 978-0-7565-2448-7 (library binding)
  ISBN-10: 0-7565-2448-2 (library binding)
  ISBN-13: 978-0-7565-3167-6 (paperback)
  ISBN-10: 0-7565-3167-5 (paperback)
  1. Brown, Oliver, 1918– —Trials, litigation, etc.—Juvenile literature.
  2. Topeka (Kan.). Board of Education—Trials, litigation, etc.—Juvenile
literature. 3. Segregation in education—Law and legislation—United
States—Juvenile literature. 4. Brown, Oliver, 1918– —Trials, litigation,
etc. 5. Segregation in education—Law and legislation. 6. African
Americans–Civil rights. I. Title. II. Series.
    KF228.B76C66 2006
    344.73'0798—dc22   2006027079

CONTENTS

The Making of a Hero

Chapter

1

Oliver Brown of Topeka, Kansas, became a hero partly by choice and partly by chance. Brown was a quiet young man. He had a steady job as a welder for the Santa Fe Railroad. On weekends, he served as a part-time minister. He and his wife, Leola, had two young daughters and were expecting their third child.

Their oldest daughter, Linda, was in elementary school. Every school day began with a difficult journey. She started by walking six blocks down a busy city street. She then crossed train tracks to reach a bus stop at Quincy Avenue. She often had a long wait at the bus stop, which had no shelter from the weather. Then Linda had a half-hour bus ride to Monroe Elementary School. Charles Sumner Elementary School, on the other hand, was just a few blocks from the Browns' home.

Charles Sumner Elementary School was close to where Linda Brown lived.

Early in September 1950, Brown took Linda to the all-white Charles Sumner Elementary School to enroll her for her third-grade year. Linda waited outside with the secretary while her father went in to talk to the principal. Brown asked him to admit his daughter. The principal refused the request. He refused it because the Browns were not white—and Charles Sumner Elementary School was for white students only. As an adult, Linda recalled:

> *When the parents involved tried to enroll us in the all-white schools and we were denied, my mother explained that it was because of the color of our skin. As a child I did not comprehend what difference that could possibly make.*

The Browns were not the only family trying to enroll their child in an all-white school. In August and September 1950, 12 other African-American parents in Topeka took the same action as Oliver Brown. The parents took their children to all-white schools near where they lived and asked the schools to enroll their children. The schools refused.

The parents' action was part of a plan made by the National Association for the Advancement of Colored People (NAACP). This group helps African-Americans organize and fight for their civil rights. Oliver and Leola Brown were not NAACP members, but many of their friends were. Brown's close friend Charles Scott was one of the attorneys for the NAACP. He helped persuade Brown to join the fight for the integration of Topeka's schools.

Lucinda Todd was the first parent to sign up for the lawsuit. She was the secretary of the NAACP in Topeka. Brown and the other parents soon followed Todd. They all volunteered to help the NAACP challenge school segregation laws. These laws allowed Topeka to have segregated

Charles Scott, a lawyer who argued many cases for the NAACP, helped persuade his friend Oliver Brown to take part in the Topeka challenge against school segregation.

Lucinda Todd wanted her daughter Nancy to have music lessons, which were available at schools for white students but not at schools for black students.

elementary schools. By trying to enroll their children in all-white schools, Brown and the other 12 parents were gathering evidence that the NAACP lawyers would need in order to bring a lawsuit against segregation.

The African-American parents gave the NAACP lawyers detailed reports of how their children had

been denied enrollment. Then the lawyers worked for several weeks to prepare their case for court. The lawsuit was filed in the U.S. District Court on February 28, 1951. The title of the suit was listed as *Oliver L. Brown et al. v. Board of Education of Topeka, Kansas.* The phrase *et al.* is a Latin term that means "and others." Today the case is simply known as *Brown v. Board of Education.*

The plaintiffs in a lawsuit are the people who make the legal complaint. The defendant is the person or group against which the complaint is made. The 13 African-American parents were the plaintiffs in the lawsuit brought by the NAACP. The defendant in the case was Topeka's Board of Education. The plaintiffs were the parents of African-American children who had tried to enroll their children in all-white schools. They were Darlene Brown, Oliver Brown, Lena M. Carper, Sadie Emmanuel, Marguerite Emmerson, Shirla Fleming, Zelma Hurst, Shirley Hodison, Maude Lawton, Alma Lewis, Iona Richardson, Vivian Scales, and Lucinda Todd.

WHY BROWN?

No one knows exactly how or why the case was named for Oliver Brown. In a lawsuit with multiple plaintiffs, it is customary to name the case after the plaintiff whose name is first in alphabetical order. Oliver Brown should have been listed second, after Darlene Brown. Perhaps the lawyers chose to list him first because he was the only man among the plaintiffs. They might also have chosen him because he had a secure job, or because he was a veteran and a minister.

Oliver Brown testified only once in *Brown v. Board of Education of Topeka, Kansas.* That testimony was his last direct involvement in the lawsuit.

Brown did not talk about the case at home, at least not in front of his daughters. They later said that the lawsuit had hardly affected their childhood at all. "Work went on, school went on, church services went on and life went on," daughter Cheryl later explained.

Oliver L. Brown was the first name listed on the Brown v. Board of Education *lawsuit.*

While Brown and the other plaintiffs went on with their lives, their lawsuit made its way through the courts. The Topeka lawsuit joined other antisegregation lawsuits until the combined case represented more than 200 plaintiffs. In addition to Kansas, the plaintiffs came from Delaware, South Carolina, Virginia, and Washington, D.C.

In time, the case became a turning point in the history of the United States. *Brown v. Board of Education* settled legal arguments that had existed since the nation's birth and addressed injustices that had lasted for centuries. The NAACP's final victory in the case destroyed the legal foundation on which segregation rested. The judgment made it clear that separate schools and other facilities for black and white people were unequal and illegal.

Today Brown's name stands for hundreds of everyday heroes—courageous community activists, plaintiffs, and lawyers. Together they defied fear, challenged the laws, and forced the United States further along toward equality and justice. ◼

Education and Emancipation

Chapter

2

The legal struggle against school segregation began more than a century before Oliver Brown tried to enroll his daughter at Charles Sumner Elementary School in Kansas. The first antisegregation lawsuit to occur in the United States took place in Boston, Massachusetts, during the 1840s.

At that time, the city of Boston provided two segregated schools for African-American students. The black schools were clearly inferior to white schools. The black schools had fewer teachers. The schools needed repairs and paint, and the classrooms were small and crowded. Many children had to walk a great distance to get to school. Parents protested against these conditions, but received no help from the school board. In 1846, a group of 86 African-Americans signed a petition asking that their children be allowed to attend the same schools as white students. The school board turned down the request.

In 1849, as a challenge to the school board, an African-American printer named Benjamin Roberts took his daughter Sarah to the nearest school to enroll her for the coming school year. It was a school for white students. Sarah usually walked right by this school—and four other white schools—to get to the African-American Smith School.

The Smith School in Boston, Massachusetts, was run for and by African-Americans during the mid-1800s.

After the white school turned Sarah away, Roberts took his case to court. His lawyers were Robert Morris, an African-American lawyer, and Charles Sumner, a white leader of the abolition movement. The Massachusetts Supreme Court ruled against Roberts. The court decided that segregated schools did not violate the civil rights of African-Americans. In response to the verdict, African-Americans in Boston organized a boycott of the Smith School and launched a public campaign for school integration. The result of the 1855 campaign was the first law in the United States to prohibit segregation in the public schools.

Though slavery was legal in the South, Massachusetts, like other states in the North, had abolished slavery. Sarah Roberts and other African-Americans living there were free. But even in the free states, African-Americans were not treated equally. Most white people thought black people were inferior and did not want to associate with them in any way. In the 1800s, only a few places allowed black students to attend public schools at all. Churches and missionary societies ran the few schools that existed for African-Americans.

A NEW RIGHT FOR CITIZENS

Public schooling paid for b local and state governmen was a new idea in the 1830 and 1840s. But educatio was rapidly accepted as citizen's right—at least fc white people. The few publi schools that admitted blac students kept them apa from white students—an they almost never hire black teachers. Only a fe colleges admitted blac students. The first college fc African-Americans, Lincol University in Pennsylvania did not open until 1854.

Still, conditions in the South, where most African-Americans lived, were far worse. The South allowed slavery, and most black people in the South were slaves.

STATES' RIGHTS

Many white Americans thought of education and slavery as states' rights issues. They thought the states rather than the federal government should decide whether to allow slavery as well as how to run the public schools.

They had no rights. Hundreds of laws known as "black codes" controlled everything they did. In almost all the slave states, it was against the law for African-Americans, slave or free, to learn to read or write. It was also against the law to teach them to read. White Southerners passed such laws out of fear that slaves might read about dangerous ideas such as the abolition of slavery. It is not surprising that African-Americans came to associate education with freedom.

Conflicts between the South and the North grew worse during the 1850s and soon exploded into war. By 1861, 11 Southern states had left the United States and formed the Confederate States of America. Their rebellion started the Civil War, which lasted until 1865.

Thousands of free African-Americans fought on the Union side of the war. The Army taught many of these soldiers how to read and write. In January 1863, President Abraham Lincoln issued the Emancipation Proclamation, freeing the slaves in all the states held by the Confederacy. As Union troops occupied parts of the South, these slaves learned they were now free. The U.S. Army became responsible for the newly freed slaves. Thousands of former slaves joined with the Union troops. The federal government enlisted abolition societies and churches to help care for and educate the freed slaves. The federal government began to operate schools for them. In freedmen's schools, the Army taught both refugees and black soldiers how to read and write.

When Union troops, including many black soldiers, captured Charleston, South Carolina, and other Southern cities, they freed thousands of African-Americans from slavery.

After the Union victory, the U.S. government started the Bureau of Refugees, Freedmen, and Abandoned Lands, or the Freedmen's Bureau. This government agency started more than 1,000 schools for former slaves.

FREEDMAN'S COLLEGES

The Freedman's Bureau founded colleges to train black teachers, including the Hampton Institute (1861), Atlanta University (1865), Fisk University (1866), Howard University (1867), Morehouse College (1867), and Clark College (1869). Black veterans and graduates of the black colleges formed a new generation of leaders for the African-American community.

For more than 10 years after the Civil War, the U.S. Army occupied the defeated Confederate states in a period known as Reconstruction. Union troops, including several African-American regiments, oversaw the governments in those states. The Army operated the schools, protected private property, and tried to keep order. It was a time of upheaval and unrest, but also a time of great promise.

Just after the war ended, Congress passed the 13th Amendment to the U.S. Constitution, officially abolishing slavery in the United States. Millions of African-Americans were now legally free. However, most of them had no land, money, or possessions. Thousands of freed slaves searched the country, looking for families who had disappeared during slavery and the war.

White landowners tried to reclaim plantations and restore burned fields. Former Confederate soldiers, angry at their defeat in the war, formed groups that raided Union camps and attacked former slaves. Gang and mob violence against black people became increasingly common.

21

Congress tried to protect the newly freed slaves by passing the 14th Amendment. The first section of the amendment states that all persons born in the United States are citizens, and it promises all citizens equal protection under the law. The 15th Amendment, passed in 1870, made it clear that "all citizens" included African-Americans and former slaves. It states:

CONSTITUTIONAL PROTECTIONS

The 14th and 15th Amendments established the legal basis for many future civil rights lawsuits. Civil rights lawyers would argue that equal protection under the law required equal treatment in all public matters. They would argue that race and color could not be used to deny any civil rights, not just the right to vote.

> *The right of citizens of the United States to vote shall not be denied or abridged by the United States or by any State on account of race, color, or previous condition of servitude.*

These changes to the Constitution were especially important because the Southern states were being readmitted to the Union. In order to rejoin the nation, each rebel state had to rewrite its constitution to fit the national laws.

Congress passed new laws to back up the new amendments. The most important was the Civil Rights Act of 1875. This law decreed that all persons in the United States were entitled to the "full and equal enjoyment" of public facilities. These rights were "applicable alike to citizens of every race

Adults as well as children eagerly attended schools run by the Freedmen's Bureau. The federal government agency helped people who won freedom from slavery.

and color, regardless of any previous condition of servitude." The law, however, did not mention public schools.

Under the protection of Union troops, African-Americans living in the South claimed land for themselves, went to school, and voted. They elected black officials—even to the U.S. Congress. By 1870, all of the former Confederate states had been re-admitted to the Union. Army troops gradually left the South, with the last withdrawal of troops occurring in 1877. After that, white southerners quickly regained political and economic power, and African-Americans lost many of the gains they had made during Reconstruction.

23

Southern states and some Northern states ignored the new amendments to the Constitution and federal laws. They claimed they had the right as states to control their own citizens. Harsh new codes prohibited black people from voting, using public schools and other facilities, and even from leaving their counties. Many African-Americans could not leave anyway because they had no money. Most of them went back to working on the land.

Freedmen's Bureau schools were turned over to the states or closed. The states were supposed to provide public schools, but only a few schools were provided for African-Americans. Almost all the money from the state went to public schools for white students only. Most schools for African-Americans were private, run by missionary societies, churches, or other charities. Several great pioneers of black education started their own schools.

During Reconstruction, freed slaves took their children to school. That changed for many when the Union withdrew its last troops from the South in 1877.

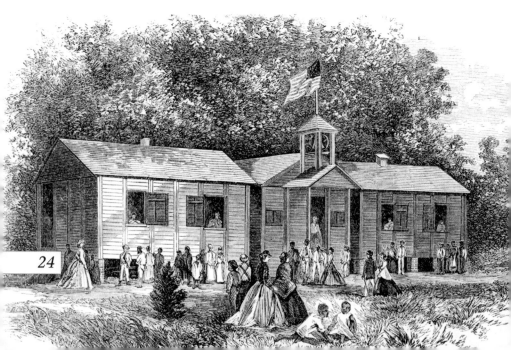

24

Many African-American families left the South—not only to escape harsh treatment and to find better jobs, but also to find better education for their children. There were many more grade schools and high schools for African-Americans in the North and West than there were in the South.

> **BOOKER T. WASHINGTON**
>
> Alabama's Tuskegee Institute is one of the earliest and most famous schools for African-Americans. It was founded in 1881, and its first president was Booker T. Washington. He was born into slavery in Virginia in 1856 and became the most widely known and influential African-American in the late 19th and early 20th centuries.

Although African-Americans had more freedom outside the South, there was still segregation, enforced by white social customs as well as by law. It was customary for African-Americans to be turned down for jobs, excluded from restaurants, theaters, and hotels, and forbidden from living in certain neighborhoods.

During the 1880s and 1890s, federal law increasingly began to support those Americans who wanted segregation. In 1883, the U.S. Supreme Court overturned the 1875 Civil Rights Act. Local and state governments quickly passed new laws in favor of segregation. Black lawyers, teachers, ministers, and other leaders challenged the unfair laws in court, but the judgments almost always went against them.

An especially important legal setback for integration came in 1896. In the case of *Plessy v. Ferguson*, the U.S. Supreme Court ruled that separate facilities for white and black people did not violate African-Americans' civil rights, as long as the facilities provided were equal. Although the case had to do with segregated seating on trains, the ruling affected many areas of public life. Moreover, states believed they now had the right to pass segregation laws.

At the start of the 20th century, African-Americans seemed to be losing ground. States passed new laws against black people. For example, South Carolina passed a law saying that people had to be able to read and write, own $300 worth of property, or pay an extra fee known as a poll tax in order to vote. These requirements prevented most African-Americans from voting. Because of similar laws, the number of African-American voters in Louisiana fell from 130,344 in 1896 to 5,320 in 1900.

THE EXODUSTERS

In the late 1870s, thousands of poor African-American farmers moved from the South to Kansas. An exodus is a great movement of people, and these people became known as Exodusters. Many of these people made the journey because they had heard the government was giving away free land. Although this report was not true, most of the Exodusters were able to build new, freer lives. They founded several all-black towns. Many got jobs with the railroads. Some of the plaintiffs in *Brown v. Board of Education of Topeka, Kansas* were descendants of these black pioneers.

SETTING A PRECEDENT OF SEGREGATION

The legal system of the United States depends heavily on precedents, or judgments made in previous lawsuits. The more often previous courts have ruled in a certain way, the harder it is for lawyers to get different rulings. *Plessy v. Ferguson* was used as a precedent to justify "separate but equal" facilities in theaters, restaurants, schools, and most public places.

Violence against African-Americans increased during this time, while in many states the number of black people who learned to read or write declined dramatically. Poverty and lack of jobs kept African-Americans down as well. In spite of these obstacles, African-Americans built strong community institutions, such as newspapers, banks, insurance companies, and especially churches and schools. The NAACP was established in 1909 by author and scholar W.E.B. Dubois and eight others. The Legal Defense Fund was established at the same time. One of the main goals of this organization was to get civil rights issues brought before the Supreme Court.

In the decades to come, all these groups would work together to change the laws that violated the civil rights of African-Americans. ◢

Strategies for Change

Chapter

3

Topeka and other cities in Kansas were favored destinations in the great migration, a massive movement of African-Americans out of the South in the late 19th century and early 20th century. World War I, which the United States fought in 1917 and 1918, created new factory jobs in Northern and Western cities.

Segregation was not as widespread in Kansas as it was in many other places. In fact, many communities had integrated schools. Zelma Hurst (later Zelma Henderson) was one of several Topeka plaintiffs who grew up going to integrated schools in tiny towns.

But even in this relatively free atmosphere, segregation and discrimination were everywhere. In Topeka, most hotels, restaurants, and movie theaters were closed to African-Americans. The public swimming pool was open to black people for only one day a year. Most black workers had low-paying jobs.

Under laws that made segregation legal, African-Americans had to use separate entrances into many public places.

In the nation as a whole, segregation became more widespread during the 1910s and 1920s. After the *Plessy v. Ferguson* ruling of 1896, institutions of all kinds felt free to refuse admission to African-Americans and to discriminate against them. Black workers were placed in segregated branches of some labor unions and kept out of others altogether. During the presidency of Woodrow Wilson (1913–1921), nearly all federal offices in Washington, D.C., became segregated. As a result, large numbers of black federal employees were fired. Public offices were also denied to African-Americans in many states, counties, and cities.

Legal segregation and discrimination against African-Americans were especially strong in the Deep South. This was a region of large cotton plantations, where the largest numbers of black people still lived. These places had harsh black codes, unfair laws that dated back to the days of slavery.

INEQUALITY OF OTHER GROUPS

African-Americans weren't the only minority group affected by segregation laws. In the Southwest, Mexican-Americans were forced to attend separate and inferior schools. In San Francisco, California, and other Western cities, there were separate schools for Asian-Americans. Native Americans were taken off their reservations and sent to church-run boarding schools far from home. They were forced to use English rather than their tribal languages and forbidden to practice their native religions.

In the 1950s, Clarendon County, South Carolina, was such a place. Eliza Briggs was a plaintiff whose lawsuit was later combined with *Brown v. Board of Education.* As a child, Eliza went to school only six months of the year. Her school, Liberty Hill, was a rickety wooden building with no desks for the students. High school for black students stopped at the 10th grade.

Because so little public money went to schools for African-Americans, the schools were often run down, poorly heated, and overcrowded.

During the 1910s and 1920s, violence against black people was on the rise, and not just in the South. Black people risked losing their jobs, being forced to move, or even being beaten or killed if they insisted on their rights. It was dangerous to join groups like the NAACP. Many black Americans felt that since segregation was a fact of life, it was better to improve segregated facilities than to insist on sharing with white people.

Oliver Brown, the plaintiff in what later became the *Brown v. Board of Education* case, was born in Topeka, Kansas, in 1918. He was one of 10 children. Like his father, Oliver grew up in an African-American community. Frank Brown, Oliver's father, worked for the railroad as a custodian. Oliver's mother cleaned houses, cooked, and did ironing.

Brown and his girlfriend, Leola Williams, and their friends were teenagers during the Great Depression of the 1930s. It was a time of deepening poverty for millions of people, and African-Americans were hit particularly hard. In Topeka and throughout the United States, there was widespread unemployment. In Clarendon County, South Carolina, and other rural areas, many families lost their farms.

During the Depression, under the leadership of the NAACP Legal Defense Fund, African-Americans stepped up legal challenges to unequal practices and segregation laws. The strategy of the Legal Defense Fund was to seek out clear examples of abuse in the existing system and to take these examples to court in order to test the laws.

Brown and Williams were married on August 2, 1939. Like many people of their generation, the couple had watched their parents struggle through the Depression. But they found their own prospects improving with the coming of World War II, which the United States fought from 1941 to 1945. Military bases and wartime industries created new jobs in Topeka and many other cities.

A LANDMARK LAWYER

In the 1930s, Charles Hamilton Houston was dean of the law school at Howard University, one of the nation's leading African-American colleges. A Harvard University graduate, Houston raised the academic standards at Howard, and he encouraged Howard to train lawyers specifically for civil rights cases. The racism he endured as an artillery officer during World War I inspired him to fight for social change. Houston became head of the NAACP's Legal Defense Fund in 1934.

After World War II, African-Americans became more outspoken in claiming their rights. During the war, they fought in segregated units and endured a great deal of racism from other troops. Conflicts between white and black workers were common in wartime factories. After the war, many black workers lost their jobs to returning white veterans. Determined black veterans added new strength to the NAACP and other civil rights organizations after the war. There were growing numbers of public protests against racism.

Legal victories were also helping to end segregation. With the support of President Harry S. Truman, several unfair housing and transportation laws were overturned. Brown and his fellow veterans won a major victory in 1948, when Truman ended segregation in the armed forces of the United States.

During the 1940s, the NAACP increased its legal attacks on inequality in labor unions, housing, transportation, and education. The leader of these campaigns was Thurgood Marshall, who became head of the Legal Defense Fund in 1938.

Thurgood Marshall, head of the NAACP's Legal Defense Fund, coordinated the efforts of legal teams that worked for civil rights in schools, public housing, and the armed services.

The NAACP began its quest to change school segregation laws by challenging law schools. Marshall and his legal team believed that cases at the university level could more easily be won. Between 1938 and 1950, the U.S. Supreme Court heard four cases between black students and law schools. In all four cases, the court ruled that law schools could not exclude black students. These victories established the legal precedents needed to challenge cases at the elementary and high school levels.

In the law school cases and other lawsuits, the NAACP lawyers argued that "separate but equal" schools were obviously not equal. Therefore the "separate but equal" law must either be enforced or abandoned. The NAACP won some cases with this argument. It became known that some judges ordered schools to be made equal to avoid having to order integration.

In 1950, the NAACP lawyers decided to shift their tactics. Instead of attacking segregation through inequality, they would tackle segregation head on. By that time Marshall and his fellow lawyers were working on two key school cases, in Clarendon County, South Carolina, and Topeka, Kansas. Both cases showed clear evidence that the phrase "separate but equal" was a fiction. Schools were not equal—and could not be as long as they were segregated. ◣

Early Cases

4

In Clarendon County, South Carolina, in the 1950s, there were good schools located close to African-American neighborhoods. The schools had modern buildings, electricity, running water, central heating, libraries, and school buses. But the good schools were for white students only. For every dollar that Clarendon County spent on the white schools, the black schools got only 24 cents.

African-American students had to walk to school, some of them as far as eight miles (12.8 kilometers). The school was a rickety wooden structure, set up on concrete blocks. There were only two classrooms—and no gym, library, or lunchroom. The school had no electricity, running water, or central heating. Each classroom had only an iron stove for heat.

The school segregation fight in Clarendon County began with a simple request for a school bus for the county's African-American schools. The Reverend Joseph DeLaine, a minister and school principal, launched a letter-writing campaign. He raised money to buy an old school bus. But the black community couldn't afford gas and repairs. DeLaine appealed in person to the district superintendent of schools. He got nowhere.

St. Paul Colored School in Clarendon County, South Carolina, was far inferior to schools for white students.

DeLaine was a member of the NAACP. In 1948, he persuaded another member, Levi Pearson, to file a formal legal petition with Clarendon County asking for buses for black students. Harold Boulware, a local NAACP lawyer, represented Pearson in the case. The suit was dismissed on a technicality.

DeLaine prepared for a new lawsuit. This lawsuit would later be the first antisegregation lawsuit to become part of *Brown v. Board of Education*.

In March 1949, DeLaine asked for help from the NAACP. Starting in March 1950, Delaine held rallies to describe the NAACP's national antisegregation campaign. That summer and fall, he persuaded 20 parents to volunteer as plaintiffs. He explained that the lawsuit would not ask just for equal schools. It would demand school integration.

Marshall, as head of the NAACP's Legal Defense Fund, went to South Carolina to work on the case. Marshall and Boulware filed *Briggs v. Elliot* in the U.S. District Court in Charleston. Harry Briggs was the first plaintiff listed on the lawsuit. R.W. Elliot was the head of the Clarendon County school board. The case of *Briggs v. Elliot* began on December 22, 1950. A panel of three judges heard the case.

In court, the NAACP lawyers presented examples of inferior classrooms and classroom materials that showed black schools were vastly inferior to white schools. This evidence proved that separate but equal schools were not in fact equal at all. Next, the lawyers argued that segregation was wrong in and of itself because it always meant inequality. To prove this point, Marshall used the testimony of psychologists and other social scientists. The

African-Americans in Clarendon County held a rally in support of integration early in 1950.

experts agreed that segregation made children feel inferior, and that feeling inferior kept children from learning.

One witness, a psychologist named Kenneth Clark, used dolls with different skin colors to find out how African-American children felt about themselves. His test showed that most African-American children thought the darker skinned dolls looked "bad." Marshall used this evidence to argue that separate schools lowered the self-esteem of African-American children.

Marshall summed up the case for the court:

> The Negro child is made to go to an inferior school; he is branded in his own mind as inferior. This sets up a roadblock in his mind that prevents his ever feeling he is equal. ... There is no relief for the Negro children of Clarendon County except to be permitted to attend existing and superior white schools.

The court ruled against the plaintiffs late in June 1951 and upheld the "separate but equal" laws. Though the judges did not order an end to segregated schools, the court did agree that black and white schools were not equal. The court gave the school board six months to come up with a plan for fixing the problem. The NAACP would have to wait six months before they could take further action.

The plaintiffs in *Briggs v. Elliot* paid a high price for taking part. Many of them lost their

jobs, businesses, or farms. Both Harry Briggs and his wife, Eliza, lost their jobs. DeLaine and his sisters were fired by the school district. A white mob shot at Delaine's house and forced him and his family to flee the state. Later their house was burned to the ground.

The NAACP's Legal Defense Fund had a better chance of winning in Topeka, Kansas, than it did in

Dr. Kenneth B. Clark, a psychologist, asked African-American students questions about black and white dolls to determine how the children felt about themselves.

41

South Carolina. Topeka's segregation was by custom more than by law. Its junior high schools had been integrated since 1941, and its high schools had always been integrated. Black people in Topeka were also more likely to escape persecution for having taken part. That expectation was fulfilled: The Topeka plaintiffs endured some public taunting, but they did not lose their jobs.

Because of segregation, the African-American plaintiffs in Briggs v. Elliot *had to sit in the courtroom balcony to watch the progress of their case.*

The case started with McKinley Burnett, the head of the Topeka NAACP chapter. In 1948, while Joseph DeLaine was filing his first lawsuit in South Carolina, Burnett was petitioning the Topeka school board, asking for an end to segregation. His petitions got nowhere.

Like DeLaine, Burnett learned about the NAACP's national antisegregation plan and began recruiting

43

parents to become plaintiffs. Their first task would be to try to register their children in all-white schools. Lucinda Todd, Oliver Brown, and the other Topeka plaintiffs challenged the law during the summer and fall of 1950.

Brown v. Board of Education of Topeka, Kansas came to trial in the U.S. District Court on June 25, 1951— right after the NAACP defeat in South Carolina. The lawyers argued in front of three federal judges. The NAACP arguments were similar to those used in South Carolina. The lawyers presented evidence that so-called "separate but equal" schools were not in fact equal. The lawyers also argued that segregation always meant inequality.

Lawyers used the plaintiffs' testimony to show that Topeka's schools were not equal. Brown described how much farther his daughter had to travel to school, just because she was not white. Todd described her attempts to get music education for her daughter that was as good as that offered in white schools. Other parents complained that black schools in Topeka had outdated textbooks. To attack segregation itself, psychologists and other social scientists testified that being set apart harmed African-American students.

The judges handed down their decision in the Topeka case in early August 1951. The judgment was against Brown and the other plaintiffs. The court upheld the practice of segregation in

Topeka's elementary schools. Although the Kansas case was another defeat for the NAACP, it was not a total loss because of how the ruling was made.

The judges had a document called Findings of Fact, which listed the legal testimony or evidence that the judges accepted as true in the case. The Findings of Fact in *Brown v. Board of Education* repeated the opinions of the psychologists and social scientists. The Kansas court stated, "Segregation of white and colored children in public schools has a detrimental effect upon the colored children."

In other words, a federal court had accepted as fact that segregation caused harm to African-Americans. This finding gave the NAACP lawyers ammunition for appealing the case to the U.S. Supreme Court. The South Carolina and Kansas battles had been lost, but the war to end segregation was far from over. ◣

THE APPEALS PROCESS

The justice system of the United States allows plaintiffs more than one chance to have their cases heard. Most cases are heard first in county or state courts. Some are heard first in federal district courts. If the plaintiffs do not agree with the verdict, they can appeal to a higher court. The judges on the higher court review the facts of the case. They then either accept or reject the appeal. Lawyers can keep appealing to higher courts until the cases reach the Supreme Court, the highest court in the land. Only the Supreme Court can overturn its own decisions.

More Civil Rights Heroes

During 1950 and 1951, while the NAACP fought and lost school segregation battles in South Carolina and Kansas, other arguments over segregation were taking place. Segregation cases were being heard in Washington, D.C., Virginia, and Delaware. Eventually those lawsuits would be combined with *Brown v. Board of Education.*

In Washington, D.C., African-American students attended overcrowded schools in poor condition, often located in poor neighborhoods. African-American schools in the city lacked books and supplies. White students had a brand new high school and other high schools and grade schools that were modern and fully equipped. While the black schools were seriously overcrowded, some of the white schools had empty classrooms. In spite of this, white and black students were kept apart.

A local barber, Gardner Bishop, led the African-American community's quest for better schools. As the parents in South Carolina and Kansas had done, Bishop and his group tried petitions and protests to help bring about change. They got nowhere. As a result, Bishop consulted a lawyer. His name was James Nabrit Jr. This was not an official NAACP case, but Nabrit followed the NAACP's strategy. He urged Bishop to demand not just schools of equal quality, but an end to segregation itself.

The well-organized campaign against segregated education in the Washington, D.C., public schools included peaceful protests as well as lawsuits.

In the fall of 1950, Bishop led a group of black students to the new, all-white John Philip Sousa Junior High School. The students asked to be admitted and were refused. Bishop had expected the students' requests to be turned down.

After the school denied them admission, the students met with Nabrit and another lawyer, George Hayes, to record what had happened. Nabrit and Hayes then filed a lawsuit demanding an end to segregated schools in Washington, D.C. The suit was named for Spottswood Bolling Jr., one of the five student plaintiffs, and for C. Melvin Sharpe, the president of the District of Columbia Board of Education.

Nabrit filed *Bolling v. Sharpe* early in 1951. In April 1951, the judge dismissed the case. He said that there was no way the court could grant relief to the plaintiffs because the law allowed segregation. Nabrit began planning his appeal to the U.S. Supreme Court.

Meanwhile, in Delaware, two cases arose during the 1950–1951 school year. New Castle County includes the city of Wilmington, its suburbs, and nearby small towns. To get to school, African-American students in the suburb of Claymont had to ride past the all-white high school and then 10 more miles (16 km) into a poor section of the city. Their school, Howard High School, was the only black high school in the state.

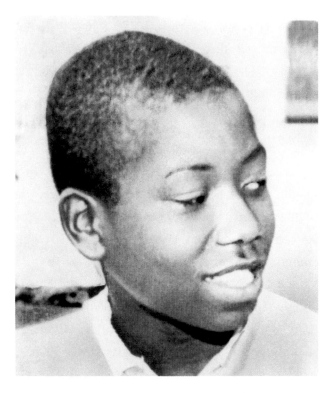

The Washington, D.C., case was named for Spottswood Bolling Jr., one of the five students who were plaintiffs in the lawsuit.

In March 1951, a group of eight parents from Claymont asked lawyer Louis Redding for advice. At his urging, the parents tried to enroll their children in Claymont's all-white school. As expected, the school turned down all the parents.

Sarah Bulah, from the small town of Hockessin, Delaware, consulted Redding at about the same time. She was angry because she had to drive her daughter two miles (3.2 km) to school, even though the school bus for the white school went right by her house. Redding persuaded Bulah to file a lawsuit demanding that her daughter be admitted to the white school.

Two lawsuits, *Belton v. Gebhart* and *Bulah v. Gebhart*, were filed in Wilmington, Delaware, in March 1951. Francis B. Gebhart, the defendant named in both lawsuits, was a member of the local board of education—her name was the first in alphabetical order.

In the fall of 1951, the two Delaware lawsuits were heard together before the Court of Chancery, the highest court in Delaware. A single judge, Collins Seitz, heard the two lawsuits, which had been combined into one case. As in South Carolina and Kansas, the NAACP lawyers used social scientists and psychologists as witnesses. The experts testified that being segregated made African-American students feel inferior, which affected their ability to perform in school. During the case Seitz also visited black and white schools to see for himself whether the schools were unequal.

Early in April 1952, Seitz ruled for the plaintiffs. He ordered that black students be admitted to all-white schools. But he would not rule against *Plessy v. Ferguson*, the landmark case from 1896 that had set the precedent for "separate but equal" laws. Seitz said that only the U.S. Supreme Court could overturn such an important precedent. Both the NAACP and the school board appealed Seitz's decision.

In Prince Edward County, Virginia, Robert Moton High School was the only high school for black students. The run-down school was built for 180 students, but in 1950, about 450 students crowded its classrooms. The county had promised a new school, but so far the school board had only built temporary classrooms that were wooden shacks covered with tar paper and heated with pot-bellied stoves. White students in Prince Edward County, however, attended Farmville High School, which was clean, modern, and well equipped.

Barbara Rose Johns, a 16-year-old student at Moton High, decided she had to act. She persuaded other student leaders to help her stage a student strike at her school. The secret strike committee made careful plans.

On April 23, 1951, the principal was called out of school to a nonexistent emergency. Barbara and the other leaders called a student assembly. The students agreed to go on strike—to stay out of class until construction had started on the promised new school.

The only school for African-Americans in Prince Edward County, Virginia, was Robert Moton High School. It had no gym, no cafeteria, and no student lockers.

Later one of the members of the strikes recalled:

> *We had 450-plus kids, ready to go. It was interesting. I mean, they were fired up. ... It was really a relief when those students jumped up and screamed and hollered and said, "Yes, we're going out." You know, it was a cheer. The cheer went like this: "Two bits, four bits, six bits, one dollar. All for the strike stand up and holler."*

The students then contacted the Virginia NAACP to ask for legal advice. In November 1951, the NAACP filed a suit in U.S. District Court, on behalf of 117 high school students. *Davis v. the School Board of Prince Edward County* asked that the court strike down the state's school segregation laws. The suit was named for its first defendant, Dorothy Davis. Barbara Rose Johns was not one of the plaintiffs. Afraid for their daughter's safety, her parents had sent her out of state to live with an uncle.

The hearing in *Davis v. School Board* started in late February 1952. The case was decided early in March. The judges upheld Virginia's segregation laws, but ordered the state's school boards to make black and white schools equal.

In November 1951, the NAACP lawyers filed an appeal with the U.S. Supreme Court challenging the *Brown* decision from Topeka, Kansas. In May 1952, they appealed the decision in *Briggs v. Elliot*, the South Carolina case. Then, in July 1952, the NAACP appealed the Virginia case, *Davis v. School*

MORE CIVIL RIGHTS HEROES

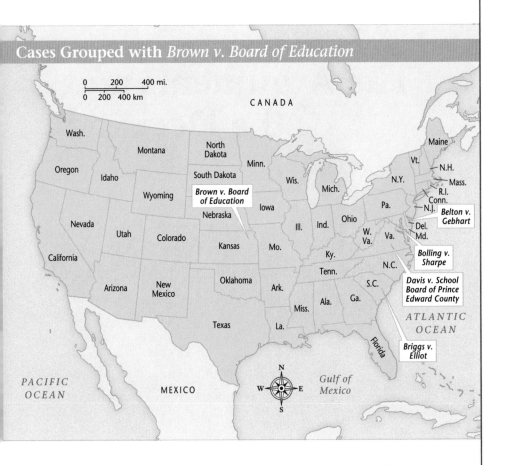

Cases Grouped with *Brown v. Board of Education*

0   200   400 mi.
0 200 400 km

CANADA

Wash.
Oregon
Idaho
Montana
North Dakota
South Dakota
Minn.
Wis.
Mich.
N.Y.
Maine
Vt.
N.H.
Mass.
R.I.
Conn.
N.J.

Wyoming
Brown v. Board of Education
Nebraska
Iowa
Ill.
Ind.
Ohio
Pa.
Belton v. Gebhart

Nevada
Utah
Colorado
Kansas
Mo.
W. Va.
Va.
Del.
Md.

California
Arizona
New Mexico
Oklahoma
Ark.
Ky.
Tenn.
N.C.
Bolling v. Sharpe

Davis v. School Board of Prince Edward County

S.C.
Miss.
Ala.
Ga.

Texas
La.

ATLANTIC OCEAN

Florida
Briggs v. Elliot

PACIFIC OCEAN

MEXICO

Gulf of Mexico

N W E S

Board of Prince Edward County. That summer, an appeal was also filed in *Bolling v. Sharpe*, the case from Washington, D.C.

The Supreme Court decided to hear all the cases at once. Later the court announced that it also would hear the Delaware cases that had been combined into one lawsuit. Now all the school segregation lawsuits were combined under the name *Brown v. Board of Education.* Oliver Brown headed a list of more than 200 plaintiffs. Soon his name would come to the attention of the highest court and of the whole nation.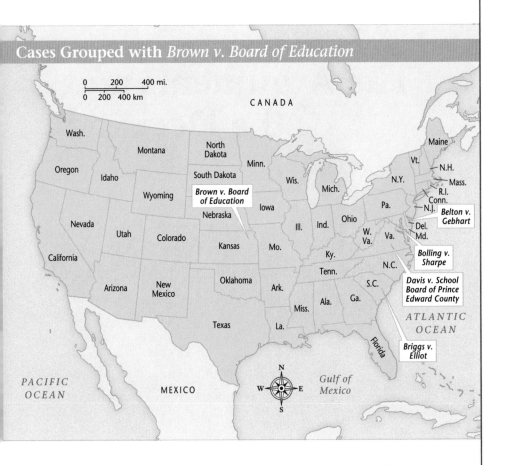

The cases grouped with Brown v. Board of Education *came from the East, South, and Midwest.*

53

The Arguments and the Decision

6

The NAACP lawyers and their opponents spent the summer and fall of 1952 preparing their arguments for the Supreme Court. Marshall was the chief counsel, or lead lawyer, for the NAACP team.

It was a presidential election year. That summer and fall, the Democratic and Republican candidates were cautious in their comments on race and school integration. Both sides were pleased that the court had set the hearing date for December, so the case wouldn't be decided until the election was over. Dwight Eisenhower, a Republican, became president that November.

The U.S. Supreme Court heard the arguments in *Brown v. Board of Education* from December 9 to December 11, 1952. People on both sides of

Hundreds of African-Americans and other supporters of civil rights lined up to hear the arguments in Brown v. Board of Education, *knowing that the court's decision would decide the future of segregation in the public schools.*

the segregation issue recognized that the court's decision would be a legal landmark. After all, the Supreme Court was being asked to do something it rarely did—overturn one of its own decisions, the *Plessy v. Ferguson* decision.

Appearing before the U.S. Supreme Court is a high point in an American lawyer's life, and it was especially exciting for the lawyers in *Brown v. Board of Education*. Lawyers from all five cases got their chance to speak, with each lawyer's time limited to one hour, including the time spent answering questions from the Supreme Court justices.

The case from Topeka—the original *Brown v. Board of Education of Topeka, Kansas*—was the first case heard by the Supreme Court. Robert Carter argued for the plaintiffs. Next came Thurgood Marshall, arguing the South Carolina case, *Briggs v. Elliot*. Spottswood W. Robinson III argued for the plaintiffs in *Davis v. School Board*, the case from Virginia. George Hayes and James Nabrit Jr. argued *Bolling v. Sharp*. Louis Redding and Jack Greenberg argued the Delaware case, *Belton v. Gebhart*.

In each case, lawyers from the other side also argued. These lawyers represented the states and district in which the cases were first filed: Delaware,

SUPREME COURT CASES

Proceedings at the Supreme Court are very formal. Cases are scheduled months in advance. Lawyers must make concise and persuasive summaries of their cases during their limited time to speak. The lawyers may also submit documents, such as decisions and Findings of Fact from the lower courts. After the hearing, the justices study the documents, debate the key points of the case, and decide on a ruling. This deliberation can take days, weeks, or months. Most of the communication between Supreme Court justices is in writing. The justices are always working on multiple cases. Debate on any one case must be scheduled carefully and limited in time.

Kansas, South Carolina, Virginia, and Washington, D.C. The states and the District of Columbia defended their right to decide policies of segregation and public education.

One of the most eloquent arguments on the civil rights side came from James Nabrit Jr. He said:

> *You either have liberty or you do not. When liberty is interfered with by the state, it has to be justified, and you cannot justify it by saying we only took a little liberty. You justify it by the reasonableness of the taking. We submit that in this case, at the heart of the nation's capital, in the capital of democracy, in the capital of the Free World, there is no place for a segregated school system. This country cannot afford it, the Constitution does not permit it, and the statutes of Congress do not authorize it.*

When the Supreme Court heard *Brown v. Board of Education* in 1952, Fred M. Vinson was the chief justice of the United States. Under Vinson, the Supreme Court was divided into factions. The justices disagreed in *Brown v. Board of Education,* and the court's deliberations lasted for a long time.

One faction, led by the chief justice, did not want to overturn *Plessy v. Ferguson.* This group supported states' rights. Some of them agreed with the idea of separate but equal. They thought that not enough evidence had been presented that segregation was against the Constitution.

Other justices supported the plaintiffs. These justices thought that *Plessy v. Ferguson* should be struck down. They agreed that separate education harmed black children and was therefore unequal. All the justices worried about the effects of school desegregation on society.

The justices were unable to agree on a decision in *Brown v. Board of Education* during the 1952–1953

Thurgood Marshall (right) and Spottswood W. Robinson III were two of the five lawyers who argued the combined case of Brown v. Board of Education *before the Supreme Court.*

58

term. In June 1953, at the end of the term, they agreed to delay the case. Justice Felix Frankfurter prepared questions for lawyers on both sides. The questions were about whether the 14th Amendment covered school segregation and how integration should be put into effect. Frankfurter asked the lawyers to research the questions and have the answers ready by the fall of 1953.

The NAACP lawyers then faced a new challenge—how to pay for more research. The lawyers had already donated thousands of hours of their own time. NAACP members and supporters made many sacrifices to pay the fees of more than 200 lawyers, social scientists, legal scholars, and historians.

Then, early in September 1953, Chief Justice Vinson died unexpectedly of a heart attack. President Eisenhower's choice to replace him was Earl Warren, the Republican governor of California. Most people expected Warren to rule against the NAACP. Because the court was evenly divided, the supporters of segregation now thought victory was near.

BECOMING A SUPREME COURT JUSTICE

Supreme Court justices are nominated by the president of the United States and then confirmed by the Senate. Justices are appointed for life. The chief justice of the United States heads the judicial branch of government, the branch that deals with the court system. In addition, the chief justice presides over the Supreme Court.

Chief Justice Warren started presiding over the court on October 5, 1953. The arguments in *Brown v. Board of Education* resumed on December 7. At this second hearing, the lawyers answered the questions the court had asked at the end of the first hearing. Robinson, Marshall, and Greenberg spoke for the plaintiffs.

The civil rights lawyers explained the history of the 14th Amendment. The purpose of the amendment, they argued, was to prevent the states from passing laws that held black people back. As Marshall put it:

Earl Warren, the chief justice of the United States, worked hard behind the scenes to resolve conflicts between the justices so that the court could issue a unanimous decision in Brown v. Board of Education.

[The Southern states were determined] that the people who were formerly in slavery, regardless of anything else, be kept as near this stage as possible. ... And now is the time, we submit, that this court should make it clear that that is not what our Constitution stands for.

As the court deliberated during the winter of 1953–1954, Warren worked hard to unite the court. He wanted the justices to be unanimous in a decision as important as this one. All the justices were aware that their decision would affect millions of American families. No matter which way they ruled, the justices saw potential lawsuits and social problems ahead. By May, Warren and Frankfurter had worked out a decision that satisfied all nine members of the court.

On Monday, May 17, 1954, the Supreme Court started its day as usual. There were rumors that something big was about to happen, but the court opened at noon with some routine cases. Then the chief justice made a surprise announcement: The court was about to deliver its decision in *Oliver L. Brown v. Board of Education of Topeka, Kansas.* Reporters dashed for the telephones to spread the news.

Warren began reading the decision at 12:52 P.M. His ruling began with a summary of the arguments on both sides of the case. He gave the court's opinion that the 14th Amendment did not address the issue of school segregation. After all, he noted, the Southern states had few public schools at all in 1868, the year the amendment was passed. But, the chief justice continued, *Plessy v. Ferguson* did not address school segregation either. He said:

> *We cannot turn the clock back to 1868, when the Amendment was adopted, or even to 1896, when* Plessy v. Ferguson *was written. We must consider public education in the light of its full development and its present place in American life throughout the Nation.*

Then the chief justice of the United States repeated the central question of the case:

> *We come then to the question presented: Does segregation of children in public schools solely on the basis of race, even though the physical facilities and other "tangible" factors may be equal, deprive the children of the minority group of equal educational opportunities? We believe that it does.*

The Supreme Court had ruled that racial segregation in public schools denied African-Americans equal protection under the law. The court also agreed that separate schools harmed black children both academically and psychologically. The ruling contained a paragraph that repeated the U.S. District Court's original ruling in *Brown v. Board of Education of Topeka, Kansas*. The wording in the paragraph used the testimony of the NAACP's psychologists almost word for word:

Segregation of white and colored children in public schools has a detrimental effect upon the colored children. The impact is greater when it has the sanction of the law; for the policy of separating the races is usually interpreted as denoting the inferiority of the Negro group. A sense of inferiority affects the motivation of a child to learn. Segregation with the sanction of law, therefore, has a tendency to retard the educational and mental development of Negro children and to deprive them of some of the benefits they would receive in a racially integrated school system.

After the Supreme Court's decision in Brown v. Board of Education, *reporters rushed to the NAACP Legal Defense Fund office in New York to interview Thurgood Marshall, the lead attorney in the case.*

Warren then made the court's position absolutely clear: "We unanimously conclude that in the field of public education the concept of 'separate but equal' has no place. Separate educational facilities are inherently unequal."

Many people in the courtroom, including some of the justices, shed tears as the chief justice read the decision. Everyone present realized they were witnessing a great moment in American history.

Nettie Hunt sat on the steps of the Supreme Court and explained to her daughter why the Brown v. Board of Education decision was so important.

The Supreme Court had ruled that complete integration was the only way to achieve equal protection. The "separate but equal" idea, on which so much discrimination had been based, had lost its power as a legal precedent.

Marshall was in New York that afternoon. When he heard the news, he later said, "I was so happy I was numb."

MIXED REVIEWS

The civil rights victory made huge headlines and brought the debate over segregation into every community and home. *The New York Times*, the nation's leading newspaper, praised the justices as "guardians of our national conscience." *The Washington Post* called the decision "a new birth of freedom." Harry F. Byrd, a U.S. senator from Virginia, however, called the decision "the most serious blow that has yet been struck against the rights of the states."

In Topeka, Kansas, Brown's wife, Leola, was at home, ironing and listening to the radio. When she heard the news, she recalled:

> *I think I was doing the dance there at home by myself. I was so elated. I could hardly wait until my kids and my husband got home. ... When they came home we had a hallelujah time that night.*

The NAACP lawyers had won a great victory for civil rights. But their triumph was not complete. Warren had worked for a 9–0 decision by the court and had gotten all the justices to agree by allowing time for integration to take place. The court's ruling in *Brown v. Board of Education* would not apply to the 1954 school year. Instead, the lawyers would

Three NAACP attorneys, (from left) George E.C. Hayes, Thurgood Marshall, and James M. Nabrit, congratulated each other after the Supreme Court declared segregation in public schools to be unconstitutional.

come back during the court's 1954–1955 term. This time the lawyers would argue about how and when to put integration into practice. Since the court's ruling would affect all the states, any state was allowed to take part in this phase of the decision. Arkansas, Florida, Maryland, North Carolina, Oklahoma, and Texas joined the lawsuit to argue in favor of states' rights—and segregation.

The NAACP legal team spent another summer deep in research. They contacted school systems that had already integrated to discover what problems schools could expect. They consulted psychologists and other social scientists to find out how to help students and teachers adjust to integrated situations. They prepared plans and arguments for total, immediate integration by order of the Supreme Court.

The Supreme Court's hearing on the timetable for integration did not take place until April 11, 1955. At the hearing, Marshall and other NAACP lawyers argued that integration should take place without delay. Marshall urged the court to move quickly and assert the power of federal law over laws of the states. The lawyers for the states argued that the schools and local governments needed time to make plans and put them in place.

The court issued its decision on May 31, 1955. To the NAACP's disappointment, the decision did not order immediate integration. Instead, the court left the manner and scheduling of integration up to the states. It ordered state and local governments to integrate "with all deliberate speed." For some years to come, Americans would be arguing about the meaning of that phrase. ◣

The Aftermath

7

The Supreme Court's decision in *Brown v. Board of Education* was like an explosion. Its shock waves spread out in all directions, into every community in the country.

Every school system now had to decide when and how to integrate. Many school systems decided to integrate immediately, without waiting for more court decisions. The public schools of Washington, D.C., and Topeka, Kansas, began integrating in September 1954. Other communities integrated on their own after the court ordered schools to do so in its May 1955 decision.

The Supreme Court had ordered integration to proceed "with all deliberate speed." The opponents of integration, however, wanted

Schools across the country began to integrate after Brown v. Board of Education *was decided.*

THE BROWNS AFTER THE DECISION

The Brown family had moved to North Topeka in 1952. They moved back to their old neighborhood in 1955. By then, Linda Brown was in junior high school, so she went to a school that had integrated long before the lawsuit demanded it. Cheryl and Terry Brown, Linda's younger sisters, enrolled in the Charles Sumner Elementary School. The school was no longer for white students only.

to make that speed as slow as possible. Southern governors and members of Congress vowed to fight the *Brown v. Board of Education* decision in the courts. One favorite stalling tactic of the states was to pass new segregation laws, which then had to be challenged in court. This tactic delayed integration in many places well into the 1960s. Public schools in Clarendon County, South Carolina, were not integrated until 1965.

In many communities, white people reacted to *Brown v. Board of Education* with hatred and violence. White hate groups targeted African-Americans who belonged to the NAACP or who spoke out for civil rights.

In spite of this opposition, *Brown v. Board of Education* breathed life and energy into the civil rights movement. For the first time, African-Americans and other minority groups realized that they could sometimes get justice under the laws. As a result, they renewed and expanded their work toward equality.

For integration to succeed, segregation laws would have to be challenged. African-Americans in every community would have to find the courage to be the first to register in an integrated school, to enter an all-white classroom, to face a hostile all-white crowd. The NAACP needed its everyday heroes more than ever.

In Baltimore, Maryland, protests by white parents tried to prevent school boards from following the Supreme Court's orders to integrate the schools.

71

Rosa Parks of Montgomery, Alabama, refused to move to the back of a city bus, a courageous stand that began the year long Montgomery bus boycott.

Rosa Parks was one of those heroes. In December 1955, in Montgomery, Alabama, Parks sat down in the white section of a city bus. She refused to move to the "colored" section at the back of the bus and was arrested. The black

community's response was to stop using the city buses until the "white" and "colored" sections were gone. The Montgomery bus boycott lasted for more than a year, until the city gave in and integrated the buses.

Parks found inspiration in her actions from the Supreme Court decision in *Brown v. Board of Education*. She said:

> *You can't imagine the rejoicing among black people, and some white people, when the Supreme Court decision came down in May 1954. ... Many of us saw how the same idea applied to other things, like public transportation. It was a very hopeful time. African-Americans believed that at last there was a real chance to change the segregation laws.*

In 1957, nine African-American students became heroes as well. The students were pioneers in attending the all-white Central High School in Little Rock, Arkansas. The Little Rock school board had produced a plan to get rid of segregation gradually. The nine black students were trying to force the school board to integrate right away. Like Oliver Brown, the students had volunteered for their mission. Community leaders and lawyers from the NAACP helped the students take their stand.

Crowds of jeering white people met the black students as they tried to enter the school. Troops from the Arkansas National Guard turned the students back, claiming it was for their own protection. A federal judge ordered the students to be admitted to the school. But Arkansas Governor Orville Faubus, the Arkansas National Guard, the Little Rock police, the Central High School administration, and an angry crowd defied the federal court.

Americans watched the dramatic events in Arkansas by means of a new, live technology—

Civil rights activist Daisy Bates (top row, second from right) helped the Little Rock Nine when they tried to attend Central High School in Little Rock, Arkansas.

74

television. The brave dignity of the Little Rock Nine and the ugly behavior of their white attackers created sympathy for the civil rights cause. Growing numbers of Americans called for the federal government to support the court's ruling. Responding to public pressure, President Eisenhower ordered U.S. Army troops to escort the Little Rock Nine into Central High School. In 1958, the governor of Arkansas closed all the public schools in the state to avoid having to integrate them. This move was ruled unconstitutional in 1959, and the schools reopened and became integrated schools.

The Little Rock Nine tested the *Brown v. Board of Education* decision. That test showed that the federal government would enforce the Supreme Court's ruling. But the Little Rock crisis also proved how many barriers there were blocking genuine integration.

In 1959, Prince Edward County, Virginia, also decided to close all the public schools in the county rather than integrate them, including the brand-new high school for African-American students. White students went to private schools that were partly funded with public money. Black students got no schools at all. The public schools stayed closed until 1964.

Oliver Brown died in 1961. He witnessed only some of the changes he had helped bring about. His daughters and the other children of the plaintiffs in *Brown v. Board of Education* grew up in the civil

75

rights era of the 1950s and 1960s. Young people in Linda Brown's generation walked into coffee shops and restaurants, sat down, and asked for menus. They stayed seated after being refused service, often until local police came to haul them away. This tactic, called a sit-in, was effective not only for testing the law but also for bringing injustice to public attention.

Civil rights activists held rallies, demonstrations, and teach-ins—workshops that explained civil rights issues. Activists also launched public campaigns to register black voters, and they challenged racist election laws in court. They pushed for new laws protecting civil rights. Piece by piece, the walls of legal segregation were dismantled. The effort took many years—and the dedication of thousands of heroes whose names never made it into the history books.

EARLY DAYS OF INTEGRATION

Henry Louis Gates Jr., a leading African-American scholar and best-selling author, described going to an integrated school in West Virginia after the *Brown v. Board of Education* decision. He wrote in his book *Colored People*:

The school board had worked out all sorts of compromises to enable integration in the county to proceed. No dating, of course, no holding hands, no dancing. Not too many colored on the starting lineup of the basketball teams. ... One colored cheerleader, max. ... Give regular lectures on hygiene. Don't rock the social boat. You'll get along as long as you abide by the rules.

Brown v. Board of Education set off a national debate about what equality meant and how far government should go to ensure equality for all citizens. It changed the political landscape as well. African-Americans and other minority groups became important voters, courted by both political parties. This led to more black people being elected to public office.

After many successes in breaking down segregation, attorney Thurgood Marshall broke down one of the strongest inner barriers in 1967. That year, he became the first African-American justice to sit on the highest court of the land, the U.S. Supreme Court.

Thurgood Marshall served on the U.S. Supreme Court from 1967 until 1991.

77

African-Americans protested against inequality during the 1963 March on Washington, D.C., that drew 250,000 people.

African-American activism in the wake of the court's decision jolted other groups of Americans into demanding civil rights as well. Native Americans, Mexican-Americans, and Asian-

Americans had also endured legal segregation from white society. Women of all races had been treated unequally under the law. *Brown v. Board of Education* gave these groups a powerful legal weapon for demanding equal opportunity and treatment.

During the 1960s and 1970s, the Supreme Court issued many rulings that backed up *Brown v. Board of Education*. To comply with the court, lower courts overturned state and local laws that discriminated against women and minority groups. Legislative bodies, from town councils to the U.S. Congress, passed laws to help integration happen faster. New phrases such as the war on poverty, equal opportunity, fair employment, affirmative action, and workplace diversity entered common speech.

Within one generation, millions of Americans had demanded their rights and changed their own futures, supported under the law by *Brown v. Board of Education*. ◢

Fifty Years Later

Chapter

8

On May 17, 2004, the Brown family returned to Monroe Elementary, the formerly all-black school in Topeka. The date was the 50th anniversary of *Brown v. Board of Education*, the legal decision that had changed the nation. The occasion was the dedication of the former school as the Brown v. Board of Education National Historic Site.

Oliver Brown's widow, now Leola Brown Montgomery, was present at the celebration, as were her daughters Linda, Terry, and Cheryl. Also present were members of the president's Cabinet, including the secretary of state and the secretary of education, both African-Americans. The governor of Kansas made an appearance. So did many leaders in civil rights and education.

Montgomery remembered her first husband, Oliver Brown. She said of him:

> *He didn't see all of these things come to fruition. He would be very, very pleased, I'm sure. And he would still be out there working even though he would be an elderly man now. He would be out there working to do what he could to further the cause of his people because he believed in that.*

President George W. Bush gave the keynote address at the event. He recalled the hardships of slavery and the injustices of segregation.

Monroe Elementary School, which Oliver Brown's daughters and other African-American children attended during the days of segregation, later became a National Historic Site.

He reviewed the events of the 50 years from 1954 to 2004 and the great changes that had taken place as a result. The president's speech ended with these words:

> *America has yet to reach the high calling of its own ideals. Yet we're a nation that strives to do right. And we honor those who expose our failures, correct our course, and make us a better people. On this day, in this place, we remember with gratitude the good souls who saw a great wrong, and stood their ground, and won their case. And we celebrate a milestone in the history of our glorious nation.*

President Bush's 50th-anniversary speech was echoed at similar events around the country. There were receptions at the White House, presentations by the Congress, and seminars at universities. Many of the speakers talked about the challenges still facing African-Americans. They argued that a majority of African-Americans now lived in cities, and many white Americans had moved to the suburbs to avoid black people altogether. This so-called "white flight" changed suburban, city, and school populations. Many formerly all-white schools became all-black, just because their neighborhoods were changing.

While *Brown v. Board of Education* changed the legal status of African-Americans, their economic status was much more difficult to change. Poverty,

as well as racism, kept African-Americans segregated in the inner cities and cut off from the better housing and schools found in the suburbs.

Across the nation, the money available for mostly white public schools was still much more than was available for schools that were mostly black. Because poorly funded public schools tended to be inferior, more parents of all races were sending their children to private schools. More parents were schooling their children at home. All these trends created new challenges for people who cared about African-American schools.

At a ceremony marking the 50th anniversary of Brown v. Board of Education, President George W. Bush was joined by a choir from a church in Birmingham, Alabama, where four young girls had died in a bombing during the struggle for civil rights.

83

The anniversary celebrations of 2004 also made it obvious how many doors had been opened because of that lawsuit 50 years before.

A parade of prominent Americans filled the nation's television screens. They were lawyers, psychologists, heads of departments at universities, elected officials, and business leaders. The group included Linda Brown Thompson, Cheryl Brown Henderson, Harry Briggs Jr., Nancy Todd, and many other children whose names had appeared in the original court documents.

Cheryl Brown Henderson represented the Brown family at the 50th anniversary celebration of Brown v. Board of Education.

Many of the people who celebrated were women. There were several TV talk show hosts, including Oprah Winfrey, the owner of a media empire and one of the world's richest women. There was a woman who had been a U.S. senator, Carol Moseley Braun. Mae Jamison, a female astronaut, and Toni Morrison, winner of the 1993 Nobel Prize in Literature, also attended.

They were some of the most famous people in the United States—and all of them were African-Americans. Fifty years before, such public events would have been almost completely dominated by white men.

After many anniversary events, the TV cameras rushed to the celebrities for comments as soon as the speeches were over. All those who were interviewed said practically the same thing: "I wouldn't have been able to achieve success without *Brown v. Board of Education*." ▰

Timeline

1849

First antisegregation lawsuit filed in Boston, Massachusetts.

1861–1865

Union and Confederate states fight the Civil War.

1865–1877

Federal troops occupy former Confederate states during Reconstruction.

1865

Thirteenth Amendment to the U.S. Constitution abolishes slavery in the United States.

1867

Howard University founded in Washington, D.C.

1868

Fourteenth Amendment to the U.S. Constitution promises equal protection under the law.

1870

Fifteenth Amendment to the U.S. Constitution guarantees the right to vote to people of all races.

1875

Civil Rights Act of 1875 guarantees equal access to public facilities.

1883

Civil Rights Act of 1875 repealed.

1896

Supreme Court decision in *Plessy v. Ferguson* establishes "separate but equal" doctrine.

1909

NAACP founded.

1917–1918

United States joins World War I, which began in Europe in 1914.

1934

Charles Hamilton Houston becomes head of NAACP Legal Defense Fund.

1938

Thurgood Marshall becomes head of NAACP Legal Defense Fund.

1938–1950

Thurgood Marshall and NAACP legal team wins four key cases affecting graduate schools.

1941–1945

United States joins World War II, which began in Europe in 1939.

1950

NAACP lawyers launch direct legal attack on school segregation; Oliver Brown and other parents attempt to enroll their children in all-white schools in Topeka, Kansas.; five students in Washington, D.C., attempt to enroll at all-white John Philip Sousa Junior High School.

December 1950

Briggs v. Elliot case filed in U.S. District Court, Charleston, South Carolina.

Winter 1951

Brown v. Board of Education filed in U.S. District Court in Topeka; *Bolling v. Sharpe* filed in U.S. District Court in Washington, D.C.

Spring 1951

Two lawsuits, *Belton v. Gebhart* and *Bulah v. Gephart*, filed in Wilmington,

Delaware; judge dismisses *Bolling v. Sharpe* case in Washington, D.C.; Barbara Rose Johns and other students stage strike at Robert Moton High School, Prince Edward County, Virginia; *Briggs v. Elliot* case argued in Charleston.

June 1951

U.S. District Court upholds "separate but equal" idea and rules against plaintiffs in *Briggs v. Elliot*; *Brown v. Board of Education* comes to trial in U.S. District Court in Topeka.

August 1951

U.S. District Court upholds segregation and rules against plaintiffs in *Brown v. Board of Education*.

November 1951

NAACP lawyers file appeal in Topeka, in *Brown v. Board of Education* case.

February 1952

U.S. District Court in Richmond, Virginia, convenes to hear *Davis v. Prince Edward County*.

March 1952

U.S. District Court upholds Virginia's segregation laws in *Davis v. Prince Edward County*.

April 1952

Judge Seitz orders school integration in *Belton* and *Bulah* cases, Delaware.

May 1952

NAACP lawyers appeal the South Carolina case, *Briggs v. Elliot*, to the U.S. Supreme Court.

June 1952

U.S. Supreme Court adds *Briggs v. Elliot* and *Brown v. Board of Education* to its schedule for the coming fall.

July 1952

NAACP lawyers appeal the Virginia case, *Davis v. Prince Edward County*, to the U.S. Supreme Court.

November 1952

U.S. Supreme Court adds *Bolling v. Sharpe* and combined Delaware cases to the combined cases.

Timeline

December 9–11, 1952

U.S. Supreme Court hears arguments in combined *Brown v. Board of Education* cases.

June 1953

Justice Felix Frankfurter submits further questions to lawyers on both sides of *Brown v. Board of Education*.

June–October 1953

NAACP Legal Defense Fund organizes research project to answer Supreme Court's questions.

October 1953

President Eisenhower appoints Earl Warren of California as new chief justice of the United States.

May 17, 1954

Chief Justice Earl Warren issues Supreme Court decision in *Brown v. Board of Education*, declaring, "Separate educational facilities are inherently unequal."

May 31, 1955

Supreme Court orders states to implement its 1954 ruling "with all deliberate speed."

December 1955

Rosa Parks refuses to sit in the back of a bus in Montgomery, Alabama, an action that sparks a year long boycott of Montgomery buses.

September 1957

Nine African-American students integrate Central High School in Little Rock, Arkansas.

1959–1964

Prince Edward County, Virginia, closes its public schools rather than integrate them.

1963

Dr. Martin Luther King Jr. leads the March on Washington and delivers his "I Have a Dream" speech.

1964

President Lyndon Johnson signs the Civil Rights Act of 1964 into law.

1967

Thurgood Marshall becomes the first African-American justice of the U.S. Supreme Court.

May 17, 2004

Nationwide observances mark the 50th anniversary of *Brown v. Board of Education*.

ON THE WEB

For more information on this topic, use FactHound.

1 Go to *www.facthound.com*

2 Type in this book ID: 0756524482

3 Click on the *Fetch It* button. FactHound will find the best Web sites for you.

HISTORIC SITES

Brown v. Board of Education National Historic Site
1515 S.E. Monroe
Topeka, KS 66612
785/354-4273

The former Monroe Elementary School, which Linda Brown attended during the days of segregation, is now a museum and the headquarters of the Brown Foundation.

Robert Russa Moton High School, Prince Edward County, Virginia
John Philip Sousa Junior High School, Washington, D.C.
Little Rock Central High School, Little Rock, Arkansas

All the above schools are National Historic Sites, which can be visited both in person and online.

LOOK FOR MORE BOOKS IN THIS SERIES

The Chinese Revolution:
The Triumph of Communism

The Democratic Party:
America's Oldest Party

The Indian Removal Act:
Forced Relocation

The Japanese American Internment:
Civil Liberties Denied

The Progressive Party:
The Success of a Failed Party

The Republican Party:
The Story of the Grand Old Party

The Scopes Trial:
The Battle Over Teaching Evolution

89

A complete list of **Snapshots in History** titles is available on our Web site: *www.compasspointbooks.com*

Glossary

abolition
the immediate ending of something, such as slavery

appeal
a formal request to try a lawsuit again, in a higher court

black codes
unfair laws specifically directed against African-Americans and other minority groups

boycott
an organized refusal to do business with a person or group as a form of protest

defendant
a person, group, or organization that is being sued in a lawsuit

deliberation
a discussion and consideration of the reasons for and against a measure

detrimental
harmful

eloquent
communicating ideas and feelings powerfully and convincingly

faction
a group of people who take the same side in a dispute

freedman
a person who had been freed from slavery

integration
the practice of making schools and other public places equally accessible to people of all races

petition
a formal request addressed to a governing body, signed by people who agree with the request

precedent
an example for future events

plaintiff
a person or group of people who file the complaint in a lawsuit

segregation
the practice of separating people of different races

technicality
a small inconsistency, such as the wrong address, that is used as a reason to dismiss a lawsuit

unanimous
agreed upon by all parties

verdict
the judgment of the court in a lawsuit

Source Notes

Chapter 1

Page 10, line 10: "Brown Sisters Interview." *Rossville Junior High Real History in the Real World.* 25 Jan. 2002. 3 Oct. 2006. www.kawvalley.k12.ks.us/brown_v_board/interview_browns.htm

Page 14, line 7: Anita Miller. "Living the Legacy." *Hers Kansas Magazine.* 16 May 2004. 2 Oct. 2006. www.herskansas.com/stories/051604/new_hers.brown1.shtml

Chapter 2

Page 22, line 16: United States. National Archives. "Transcript of Fifteenth Amendment to the United States Constitution: Voting Rights." *General Records of the United States Government, Record Group 11.* 3 Feb. 1870. 3 Oct. 2006. www.ourdocuments.gov/doc.php?flash=true&doc=44&page=transcript

Page 22, lines 28 and 30: "Civil Rights Act of 1875." *TeachingAmericanHistory.org.* 18 Oct. 2006. http://teachingamericanhistory.org/library/index.asp?document=481

Chapter 4

Page 40, line 13: Richard Kluger. *Simple Justice: The History of Brown v. Board of Education and Black America's Struggle for Equality.* New York: Alfred A. Knopf, 1976, p. 363.

Page 45, line 12: Ibid., p. 424.

Chapter 5

Page 52, line 2: Martha Irvine. "Brown at 50: Landmark decision causes look back." *The Messenger Online.* 17 May 2004. 3 Oct. 2006. www.the-messenger.com/articles/stories/200405/16/016b_kystyle.html

Chapter 6

Page 57, line 7: *Simple Justice*, p. 580.

Page 61, line 1: "Script for Re-Enactment of Brown v. Board Oral Arguments," American Bar Association Division for Public Education, 2004. 30 Oct. 2006. www.abanet.org/brown/reenact.pdf, pp. 29–30.

Source Notes

Page 62, line 5: United States. National Archives. "Brown v. Board of Education of Topeka, Opinion." *Records of the Supreme Court of the United States, Record Group 267*. 17 May 1954. 3 Oct. 2006. www.ourdocuments.gov/doc.php?flash=true&doc=87

Page 62, line 13: Ibid.

Page 63, line 1: Ibid.

Page 64, line 2: Ibid.

Page 65, line 13: *Simple Justice*, p. 714.

Page 65, line 18: "Black/White & Brown: Brown versus the Topeka Board of Education." Topeka PBS affiliate (2004). 3 Oct. 2006. http://ktwu.washburn.edu/productions/brownvboard/brown60minute.pdf

Page 65, sidebar, all: *Simple Justice*, p. 710.

Chapter 7

Page 73, line 9: Gallagher and Associates. "Separate Is Not Equal: Brown v. Board of Education." *Smithsonian National Museum of American History, Online Exhibitions* (2004). 3 Oct. 2006. www.americanhistory.si.edu/brown/history/index.html

Page 76, sidebar: Henry Louis Gates Jr. *Colored People: A Memoir*. New York: Knopf, 1994.

Chapter 8

Page 81, line 3: Martha Irvine. "Reflections on Brown v. Board of Education decision—50 years later." *San Francisco Chronicle*, 15 May 2004.

Page 82, line 5: George W. Bush. "Remarks at the dedication ceremony for Brown v. Board of Education National Historic Site. " 17 May 2004. 3 Oct. 2006. http://brownvboard.org/dedication/remarks/bush.php

SELECT BIBLIOGRAPHY

Chafe, William H., Gavins, Raymond, and Korstad, Robert, eds. *Remembering Jim Crow: African Americans Tell About Life in the Segregated South.* New York: New Press, 2001.

Cottrol, Robert J., Diamond, Raymond T., and Ware, Leland B. *Brown v. Board of Education: Caste, Culture, and the Constitution* (Landmark Law Cases and American Society). Lawrence: University Press of Kansas, 2003.

Gates, Henry Louis, Jr. *Colored People: A Memoir.* New York: Knopf, 1994.

Klarman, Michael J. *From Jim Crow to Civil Rights: The Supreme Court and the Struggle for Racial Equality.* New York: Oxford University Press USA, 2004.

Kluger, Richard. *Simple Justice: The History of Brown v. Board of Education and Black America's Struggle for Equality.* New York: Alfred A. Knopf, 1976.

Patterson, James T. *Brown v. Board of Education: A Civil Rights Milestone and Its Troubled Legacy.* New York: Oxford University Press USA, 2002.

Raines, Howell. *My Soul is Rested: Movement Days in the Deep South Remembered.* New York: Putnam's, 1977.

FURTHER READING

Arthur, Joe. *The Story of Thurgood Marshall: Justice for All.* Milwaukee: Gareth Stevens Publishers, 1996.

Gold, Susan Dudley. *Brown v. Board of Education: Separate but Equal?* New York: Benchmark Books, 2005.

Horton, James Oliver. *Landmarks of African American History.* New York: Oxford University Press, 2004.

McNeese, Tim. *Brown v. Board of Education: Integrating America's Schools.* New York: Chelsea House, 2006.

Schraff, Anne E. *Booker T. Washington: Character is Power.* Berkeley Heights, N.J.: Enslow Publishers, 2005.

Treanor, Nick, ed. *The Civil Rights Movement.* San Diego: Greenhaven Press, 2003.

Index

ABOUT THE AUTHOR

Judith Conaway has been a writer and producer of educational materials for more than 25 years. She has written numerous fiction and nonfiction books in subjects ranging from history to crafts. She lives in Chicago.

IMAGE CREDITS